In *Osteoblasts to the Rescue*, Dr. Heather Manley authors  ∋
Skeletal System. Reading illustrated books with your childre   the
story reminds us that laughter is good for the immune syst
that healthy eating really does matter, that yoga is good for balance and bones, that kale tastes
great and that we all need to take care of ourselves, and each other. In her fourth book of the
Human Body Detectives series, she continues to inspire kids (and their parents!) to understand their
bodies and the value of embracing a healthy and simple lifestyle with confidence.

Lisa Borden
BORDEN COMMUNICATIONS + DESIGN Exceptional Ideas . Ethical Business

"As a Chiropractor and mother of three boys, it's truly amazing to teach children to trust in the healing
power of their own bodies! Dr. Heather has created an unparalleled, educational tool in this book.
Readers are captivated as they ride on an exciting adventure, zooming through the skeletal system,
learning fun facts, and illustrating how the body heals itself. I am grateful for the HBD Series as a
creative resource to aid parents and children in the wonderment of health."

Michelle M. Laus, D.C.

With *Osteoblasts to the Rescue*, Heather Manley once again succeeds in making science, health
and nutrition exciting and fun for kids. As a homeschooling parent, I love having such an engaging
way to teach and reinforce concepts about anatomy, medicine and the human body. From
preschooler to 5th grader, all of my kids love the *Human Body Detectives*, and we're excited to
follow Merrin and Pearl on their next adventure!

Kristie McNealy MD
Medical Researcher and Homeschooling Mom
www.KristieMcNealy.com

The more children understand something, the better they are at making good choices for themselves. Educating them to do something with a background of why and how taking that action can make them healthier and bigger and stronger is significantly more effective than simply telling them to do something. The **Human Body Detective** Book series gives children the why and how in an exciting adventure; this gives them story with a message which helps them make better health decisions for themselves. Our children are battling obesity and other health related issues that in the past were only seen in the adult population after years of poor diet and reduced exercise. They will feel the burden of chronic disease far too young if we continue on at this pace. In "Osteoblasts", the children will learn the incredible regenerative power of the body, in this case the bones, and how wonderfully our bodies heal and want to be healthy. They will learn some of the anatomy of the bones which might spur them on to think of their body's in a new way and move with more intent and strength, all helping them achieve better health and a longer, more pleasurable life.

Hilary Andrews, ND
Naturopath
Portland, OR

Human Body Detectives teaches children how their bodies work with lively, interesting stories that focus on individual systems but then connects those systems so that kids understand how their bodies really work. I love that the stories weave food and nutrition into the narrative to give kids an understanding of why eating whole foods is so important. If you're looking for something that educates and entertains children – while teaching parents as well – don't miss out on this modern "physiological" version of the Magic School Bus series.

Mel Hicks
President, Big Time Tea Company

"A terrific way to "bone up" on your knowledge of the skeletal system! Once again, Merrin and Pearl's delightful adventures allow readers to learn science and health from a new perspective."

Allison Ellis
Youth Media Consultant

Human Body Detectives is the most innovative way to teach children in making the connection between their diet and how it affects their bodies. These books are well written, so children can understand and look forward to the next adventure with excitement. Dr. Manley's mission is perfectly aligned with Vitalah's creators of Oxylent to empower children in making healthy choices to contribute to their overall good health and wellbeing. We look forward to seeing more *Human Body Detectives* at work! Thank you Dr. Manley!

Lisa Lent
Founder/CEO of Vitalah

Osteoblasts to the Rescue, part of the **Human Body Detective** Series is a lively narrative full of adventure! Dr. Heather not only simplifies the very complex human skeletal system for young readers, but also teaches them how to feed their bones, too! The sautéed kale and apple recipe definitely gets a thumbs up from me! I love when anatomy and nutrition get served up together with edamame soybeans and sesame seeds – common sense healthy eating – well done!

Stacey Antine
MS, RD, founder, HealthBarn USA, author, Appetite for Life.

Dr. Manley finds the perfect balance between education and entertainment in Osteoblasts to the Rescue. The book captured my attention from the first to the last page. Throughout Pearl and Merrin's incredible journey, I found myself intrigued by the rib cage, what to eat to make sure my bones stay strong, and the magical healing power of osteoblasts. Dr. Manley even ends the book with fun facts and jokes about our skeletal system, making sure to offer a little fun education for every kind of learner.

Skylor Powell, CHC
www.sprouthealthlifestyle.com

Heather Manley, N.D.
www.drheathernd.com

Copyright © 2013 by Heather Manley, N.D.
All rights reserved. Printed and published in the United States of America.

No part of this book may be used or reproduced
in any form without written permission from the author.

For reproduction of any part of this book
or for more information please contact:
Heather Manley, N.D.
email: drheather@drheathernd.com
www.drheathernd.com | www.humanbodydetectives.com

human body detectives®

Osteoblasts
to the Rescue

CASE FILE #4

Dr. Heather Manley

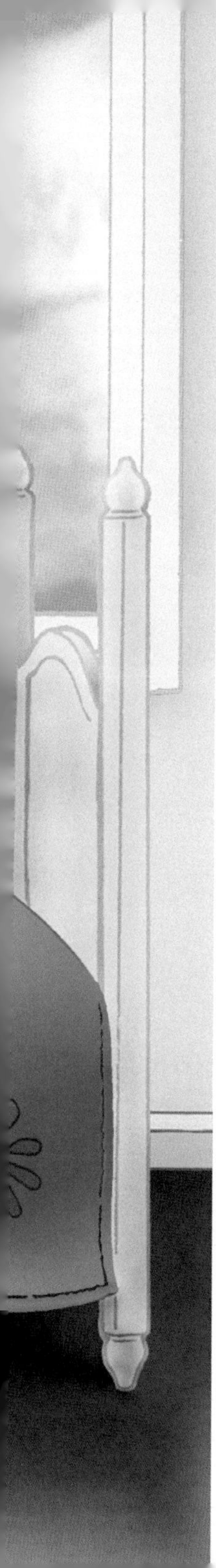

It was a bright and sunny Saturday afternoon, but Pearl sat in her room alone, deep in thought.

"206," she muttered. "I don't understand. How could there be just 206 in the human body? They give us strength and let us stand upright, so why only 206?"

Not being one to contain her curiosity any longer, Pearl screamed to her sister.

"*MERRINNNNNNN!*"

"Pearl, why so loud? I'm right here," Merrin replied.
She walked into Pearl's room and plopped down on her bed.

"*What's up?*"

"This book says there are only 206 in the body and it doesn't seem right. I have to get in a human body to find out for myself... now."

Merrin sighed and reminded her that they were going to their friend and neighbor Ben's soccer game. *We do have the gift of going into other people's bodies to help them feel better, but being a Human Body Detective is a big responsibility and no one seems to need help right now*, Merrin thought.

After some prodding, Merrin and Pearl headed to the soccer field where they met up with their friends who were cheering for their high school soccer team.

Skye, Merrin's best friend, showed up with her cousin, Lily. As Skye introduced Lily, Pearl noticed that Lily had a very **LARGE** and very **ORANGE** cast on her left arm. She looked intensely over at Merrin who ignored her... for as long as she could.

Pearl made her way over to Merrin and placed her hand next to hers so they were barely touching. Merrin glanced over at Pearl and whispered, "No." But clearly Pearl was not concerned, knowing they would be missed for only a second or two—in real time. Pearl closed her eyes and began visualizing them inside of Lily's body.

The familiar DIZZINESS that they always felt when they were about to go on a Human Body Detective adventure settled in... but it didn't last long.

Pearl heard Merrin sigh and mutter, "Pearl..."

They landed on a hard smooth surface.

Happily, they were still together. As their eyes opened, Pearl looked around and Merrin gasped, "*PEARL, WHERE ARE WE?*"

Pearl had been reading up on the skeletal system lately. In fact, she had a school science quiz on it the following week. Pearl calmly said, "ON BONE, COMPACT BONE."

Merrin panicked.

How much does Pearl know?

Will we get lost?

"Look Merrin, you can see the periosteum. It's the layer between the skin and compact BONE.... therefore, it's the outer surface on the compact BONE. It houses nerves and blood, which feeds the BONE. Wait a second, you do realize BONE is living and needs to be fed from healthy foods we eat, right?"

Merrin didn't know that much about BONE, but she did start to feel a little more relaxed since Pearl seemed to be a master of the skeletal system. *Maybe the number 206 has something to do with the skeletal system*, she thought.

Pearl looked around. She discovered the BONE they were on had arch-like things projecting from them. "These are called spinal processes," she said. She looked up and down and noticed that the surrounding BONES were all similar.

"This isn't where we want to be. I'm pretty sure we're on the vertebrae. The vertebrae have 5 different sections: not sure where we are exactly. Could be the cervical, but I don't see the skull so maybe we're on the thoracic or lumbar—the middle part of your backbone. It's obvious we're not at the sacrum or coccyx as those BONES are fused together and don't have the spinal processes."

Merrin looked confused. Their roles had absolutely changed. Typically, she was the one who knew where they were and what they were doing when they were on a Human Body Detective adventure. Merrin asked, "The vertebrae column is also called the spine or backbone, right? But *WHAT IS A SPINAL PROCESS?*"

Pearl leaned over to Merrin and felt along her spine. Merrin SHIVERED a bit.

"Those BONES you feel when I touch your back are the spinal processes."

"Oh, okay. It feels funny when you touch them! Well, where do you want to go?"

"We need to get to Lily's left arm, the one that is broken. I want to see the break and understand how the body will fix it.
We might be in for a journey, Merrin! Most of the vertebrae have these spinal processes and if we climb up toward her head, we'll find Lily's left clavicle, which will lead us to her left arm."

Oh my, Merrin thought.

"Okay, let me think. The cervical vertebrae make up the neck and are smaller than the other vertebrae. The one we're on is bigger so I'm going to guess we're on a thoracic vertebrae. Let's start climbing up."

Merrin looked around. To climb straight up the thoracic vertebra appeared quite dangerous. She glanced around and some of what she had learned about the skeletal system vaguely came back to her.

"PEARL, I SEE THE RIBS!"

"Yes, there are 12 pairs of ribs..." Then she giggled knowing Merrin wasn't the best at math," just in case you may not understand, that equals 24 ribs."

Merrin rolled her eyes, knowing full well that math was not Pearl's best subject either. She was a whiz at science though!

Merrin continued, "The first 7 ribs are called the true ribs because they attach to the sternum by costal cartilage. Ribs 8, 9 and 10 are considered false ribs because they do not directly attach to the sternum—they kinda interconnect and then attach with rib number 7. The last 2 ribs are called floating ribs because have no attachment with the sternum, only to the thoracic spine—they just float there"

Pearl suddenly got an idea.

"It might be best if we jump to a rib, follow it to the sternum and then climb up. Once at the top, we'll be able to get to the collarbone—also called the clavicle. It is just above the first rib and attaches to the sternum."

Merrin chimed in, "*GOOD IDEA!* And I happen to know that the clavicle is the only long BONE in the body that runs horizontally, which means it will take us to Lily's left arm. Let's do it, Pearl!"

Pearl made a leap to the rib and looked up. She could see 2 ribs above them. "We are closer than I thought," she mumbled to herself. She turned to Merrin and told her to jump. Dutifully, she did.

They began to walk, very carefully, on the rib. It was skinny and they concentrated hard on each step. Merrin stretched her arms out and was thankful for the yoga classes she had been taking. Yoga helped with her balance and maybe even her BONES. Feeling confident, Pearl began to pick up the pace. Merrin realized Pearl's shoelace was untied and bellowed out,

"PEARL SLOW DOWN AND TIE YOUR SHOELACE!"

But she was too late. Pearl tripped and then... She TUMBLED.

She landed on her stomach, her feet dangling off the rib.

She tried hard to pull herself up but she was slipping.

In the blink of an eye, her legs slipped and she was hanging on with only her hands. Merrin ran over to her. Pearl's eyes were wide with fear.

"DON'T LOOK DOWN, PEARL."

She did and glanced back up to Merrin, now with pleading eyes. If she fell, she would tumble between all the ribs below and probably land, if she were lucky, on the stomach. It may be a soft landing, but it was super far from Lily's arm, where they wanted to be.

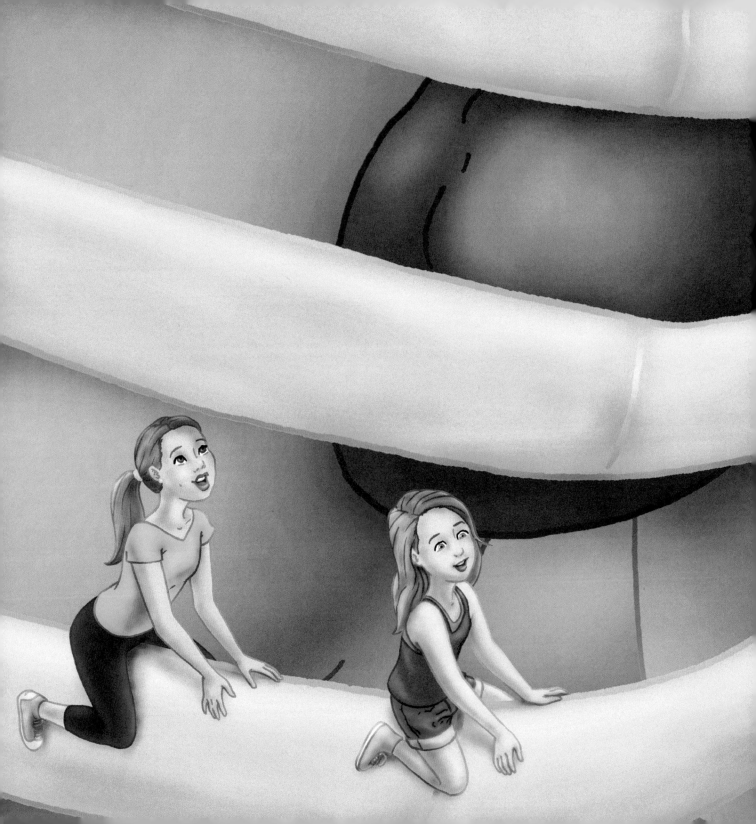

Merrin thought fast then straddled the rib to get a secure grip. She reached out her arm to Pearl. Pearl nervously grabbed it and Merrin pulled her up.

"**Phew**"

"Pearl, let's straddle the rib and slide to the end."

Pearl, still shaken up, nodded yes.

They slid down the rib curving gently to the right. They picked up speed when they spotted the end.

"I see the sternum. How can we stop?"

Pearl yelled, "We'll hit the costal cartilage first. They are a softer version of the rib BONE—it will give us a cushy landing."

The minute they hit the cartilage that bridged the rib BONE to the sternum, they stopped abruptly and clumsily—crashing into each other. They looked at each other ready to start a sibling fight, but then began to laugh ... hard.

"Remember when we were in Cousin Max's immune system on another **Human Body Detective** adventure? We learned laughing is good for the immune system. And remember Quickster and Speedy, the helpful macrophages, also known as a white blood cell?" Pearl reminisced.

"Yeah, that was a great adventure! It was fun to have Cousin Sam journey with us too. He was a great `Human Body Detective`."

Both girls quietly pondered one of their previous journeys, then they wondered how they were going to continue on their current exploration.

"If Sam were here now he would have a clever idea on how to climb up the sternum." They both looked up and noticed the sternum `BONE` was completely vertical. They would need rock climbing gear to have any chance of getting to the top.

This would require serious teamwork. Luck was on their side as it looked like they only needed to go up 2 ribs to get to the clavicle, and that was doable. Merrin, struck with an idea, kneeled, offering one of her legs for Pearl to step on. Pearl climbed up on Merrin's knee and was just tall enough to grab onto the rib above them.

Merrin hoisted Pearl up and then Pearl reached down and pulled Merrin onto the next rib with her.

Once they were at the clavicle, they collapsed and caught their breath.

"I'm hungry," said Pearl.

"How can you think about food?"

"Well, what about the food that helps bones? Minerals like calcium, phosphorus and magnesium help them. Mom talks about vitamin D being helpful, too."

"But what foods are those minerals in?" Merrin asked.

"Probably dark leafy greens like kale. I love it when mom sautés kale with apples!" Pearl answered.

"That is good, especially when she adds a few nuts!"

"Let's stop talking about food and get moving. We need to get to Lily's arm."

Merrin and Pearl carefully walked along the clavicle, being extra cautious with each step. The clavicle was a bit wider than the rib; however, they were much higher up this time. They began to feel a bit grateful for their own strong BONES, which helped them be good Human Body Detectives.

At the end of the clavicle, they noticed a big, round, white BONE just beneath them. Pearl gently r e a c h e d down to touch it and said, "Ahhh, the shoulder BONE," but she was suddenly startled when something poked her.

"My shoulder is so itchy," they heard Lily say, her voice far away.

At that moment they realized Lily was scratching her shoulder. Pearl was extremely lucky not to have been knocked down. They needed to move faster. They looked at each other and held hands.

"On the count of 3," Merrin said. "**1...2...3!**" The girls jumped down to the shoulder.

They landed and quickly realized that the jump was the easy part. They looked down and only saw one long BONE.

"What BONE is this, Pearl?"

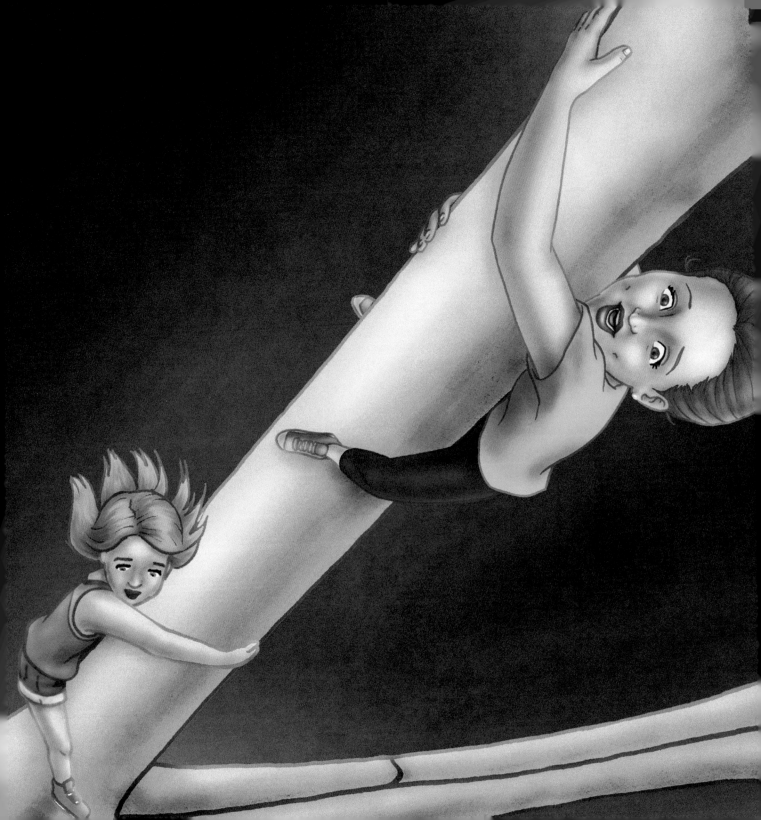

"It's the humerus BONE. Not sure how we'll get down it."
Pearl thought fast and suggested, "Hey, how about like when
firefighters twirl down their poles when their sirens go off?"

"Oh my," Merrin whispered to herself.

They both looked at each other and wondered if they were
brave enough to do it. Who knew where they would land, let
alone if they fell off the BONE? Finally realizing there was no
other option, Pearl made the first move. Merrin followed right
behind. They twisted and twirled all the way down and had a
soft yet kinda bouncy landing ... almost like on a trampoline.

Then they detected a faint noise, a giggle that seemed to
get louder.

"What's that?" Merrin questioned.

"It must be Lily. She's laughing!" Pearl responded.

Lily's laughing began to shake them back and forth and
quickly they leaned down and grabbed hold of the BONE;
they needed to get a strong grip to avoid falling.

"Why is Lily laughing? Do you think she feels us?" Merrin asked.

They heard Skye ask, "What's so funny?"

"I'm not sure... it's my elbow—it feels weird."

"Ha ha ha," Pearl giggled, "No, I don't think she can feel us, but I think we hit her funny BONE. But the funny BONE is not really a bone; it's the ulnar nerve, which helps you move a few of your fingers. We must have landed on her ulnar nerve!"

They joined in the laughter, remembering times that they had hit their own ulnar nerves.

They climbed up onto a round BONE. "We must be on the elbow BONE. Hmm, maybe this is the one of the epicondyles? There are 2 that stick out at your elbow," Pearl muttered to herself.

"Pearl, look," Merrin said, pointing her finger.

"The fracture! It's on the ulna BONE.

"Fracture?"

"The medical name for a BONE break is called a fracture."

"Ohh, good to know," Merrin said.

"The fracture appears to be a simple fracture because it doesn't break the skin surface. She must have hit it hard! Ouch."

Pearl kept talking, "There's also another kind of fracture, called a greenstick fracture, where the bone bends and cracks yet doesn't break. Let's get closer to look at Lily's break."

They s l o w l y moved down the ulna bone. They could see Lily's other forearm bone, the radius, which was a little smaller. As they approached Lily's injury, they observed lots of blood vessels surrounded by a soft red bump. Merrin had no idea what was going on.

"That bump is called a hematoma," Pearl said, reading Merrin's mind.

"It will turn into a callus, which looks like it's beginning to form. Once the callus forms, fibroblast cells come in and make collagen which is part of bone. Once the callus has more collagen, osteoblasts begin turning the callus into new bone. Super cool."

"I guess you could say the bones are natural healers!" Merrin added. Then she asked, "And Pearl, what did you mean when you kept saying the number 206?"

Pearl had no chance to answer. At that moment, osteoblasts came storming out from everywhere! They were all over the place. Merrin and Pearl tried to jump out of their way, but the osteoblasts were on a mission and didn't even notice them. They were lucky, very lucky, not to have been knocked over. They watched the osteoblasts secreting something.

"LOOK, MERRIN! The osteoblasts are releasing osteoid, or the matrix. Lily's arm is starting to heal! And once the bone matrix gets a good dose of the minerals calcium and phosphorus, new bone will be born!"

"Well, I hope Lily is eating enough foods with calcium and phosphorus. Actually, what food does she need to eat to get more of these nutrients?" Merrin asked.

"You can get calcium from spinach, sesame seeds, broccoli or almonds. Some foods that have phosphorus are sunflower seeds, soy beans and lentils."

"Okay, let's get out of here now and tell Lily to eat these foods for lunch. I'm ready to get back to the school soccer game."

"Me too, yet I am still baffled by the fact that there are only 206 bones in the human body. I have to say, bones are pretty cool!"

Ready to go back to their friends, they closed their eyes and imagined themselves at the soccer field. They felt the same dizzy, swirling sensation they always felt when they were leaving a body. The feeling suddenly disappeared and they heard cheers, whistles and claps.

Merrin and Pearl blinked their eyes open right as everyone at the soccer game jumped to their feet screaming,

"GOAL!"

Quickly, they joined in and smiled at each other. They knew once everything settled down after the game, they would invite Lily and Skye over for edamame soy beans sprinkled with sesame seeds: both delicious and high in calcium and phosphorus!

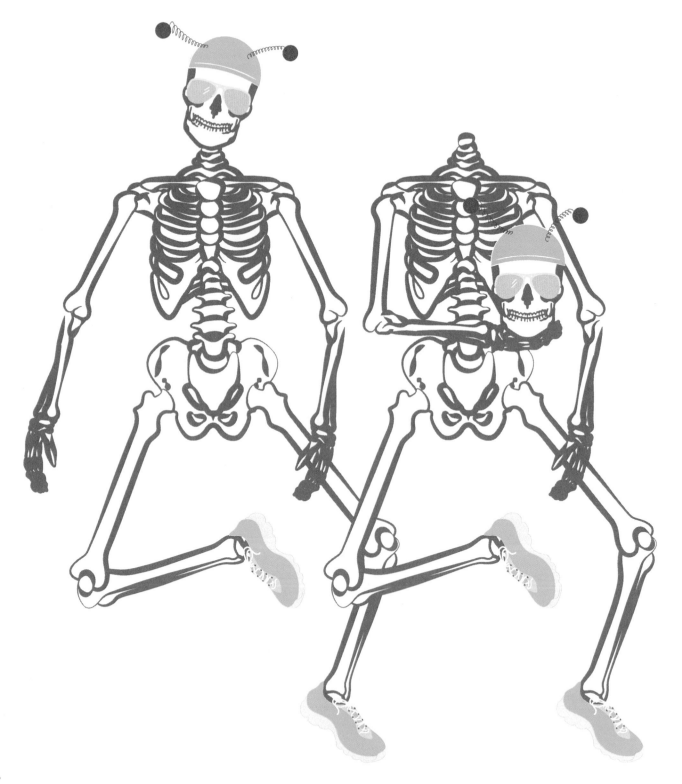

human body detectives

case solved

CASE FILE #4

How good of a detective are you?

Can you find Mr. Osteoblast?

Let us know how many times you spotted him at merrin@drheathernd.com or pearl@drheathernd.com

More About the Skeletal System

Your bones are alive!

When we are born we have 300 bones. Most of these bones are cartilage, which feels rubbery and is quite soft and flexible. Your nose and outer ear are still made up of cartilage. As we become older, the cartilage will turn into solid bone; a process called ossification. In addition to the cartilage turning into bone, many of the bones will fuse together and become one larger bone. As an adult, we will end up having 206 bones in total.

Bones come in many sizes and shapes. This allows for optimal movement and strength. And bones are the ideal shape to protect our vital organs. There are long bones in your arms and legs, shorter bones in your feet and hands, flat bones that allow muscles to attach to and protect our midsection, and then the round or sesamoid bone. The patella bone is a perfect example of a sesamoid; it's a round-shaped bone located on your knee. And curiously, nearly half of all the bones in the body are in your hands and feet!

The spine is your backbone and lets you twist and bend. The spine has the important job of protecting your spinal cord. The spinal cord is a bundle of nerves that sends messages to and from the brain.

There are 5 different types of vertebra: cervical, thoracic, lumbar, sacral and coccygeal. The cervical are the first 7 vertebrae located at the back of your neck, below your skull. It keeps hold of your very heavy brain. There are 12 thoracic vertebrae, in which 10 attach to the ribs. Below the thoracic vertebrae are the 5 lumbar vertebrae and the sacrum is made of 5 fused bones. At the bottom of the spine is the coccyx, made up of 4 bones that have fused together to form the tailbone.

In between each vertebra are small disks made up of cartilage. The cartilage acts like a pillow for the vertebrae. So every time you jump or run, the vertebrae are not bumping into and harming each other.

The thoracic vertebrae attach to 10 pairs of ribs. There are 12 pairs of ribs (24 in total) that protect your heart, lungs and liver. Ribs 1 through 7 attach directly to the sternum, or breast bone. Your sternum is located in the center of your chest. Ribs 8 through 10 indirectly attach to the sternum; they collectively join together and attach to the sternum with rib number 7. The last 2 pairs of ribs are floating ribs and do not attach to the sternum, only the thoracic vertebrae.

Joints are very important and are the places where 2 bones join together. Joints allow the bones to move. They have a special fluid called synovial fluid that helps them move freely. There are a few types of joints: fixed joints like the parieto-temporal joint (skull), which do not move; hinged joints (elbow); and ball and socket joints (shoulder). Bones are held together at the joints by ligaments, which are like very strong rubber bands.

Bones need exercise and nutritious foods to be strong and healthy. Exercise such as jumping rope and running makes bones strong. Lace up your running shoes and get outside and play! And remember to choose a variety of colorful foods. They will all have calcium, magnesium and vitamin D that will help keep your bones healthy.

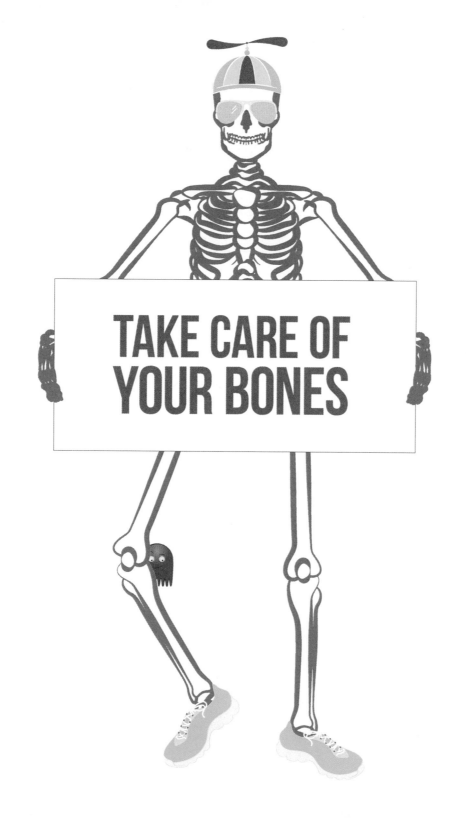

Human Body Detectives Ask You...

Pearl was intrigued by the skeletal system. She learned some fun facts along the way and wanted to share them with you.

did you know that...

your bones will stop growing when you are 25?

"osteo" is the Greek word for bone?

bones can stick around for 1,000 years before decaying?

approximately 1/7 of your total body weight is bone?

the smallest bone, the staples bone, is located in the ear?

there are 24 ribs in the human body (12 pairs)?

1 in every 200 people will have 1 or 2 extra ribs?

the skull is a collection of 22 fused bones?

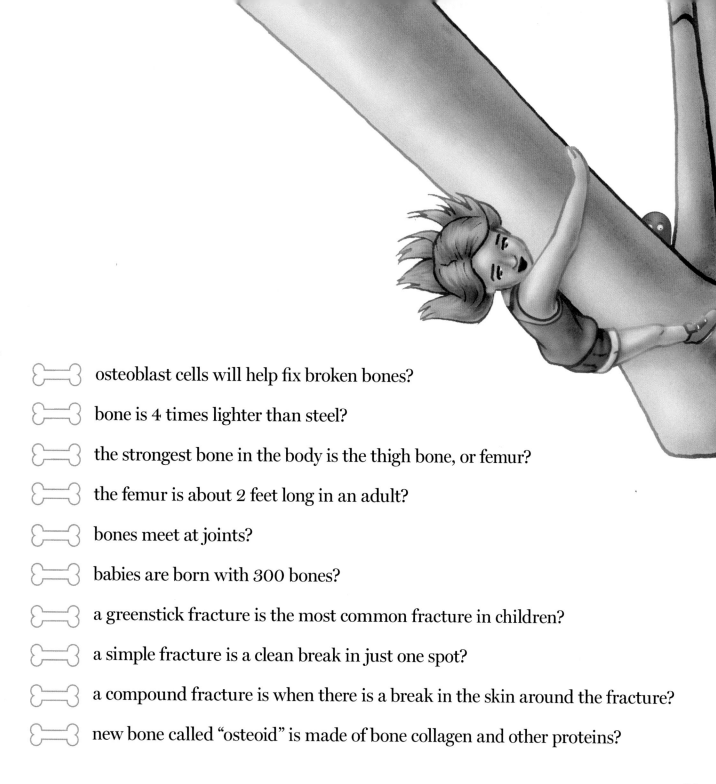

osteoblast cells will help fix broken bones?

bone is 4 times lighter than steel?

the strongest bone in the body is the thigh bone, or femur?

the femur is about 2 feet long in an adult?

bones meet at joints?

babies are born with 300 bones?

a greenstick fracture is the most common fracture in children?

a simple fracture is a clean break in just one spot?

a compound fracture is when there is a break in the skin around the fracture?

new bone called "osteoid" is made of bone collagen and other proteins?

Label Your Bones

Can you label a few bones in the skeletal system?

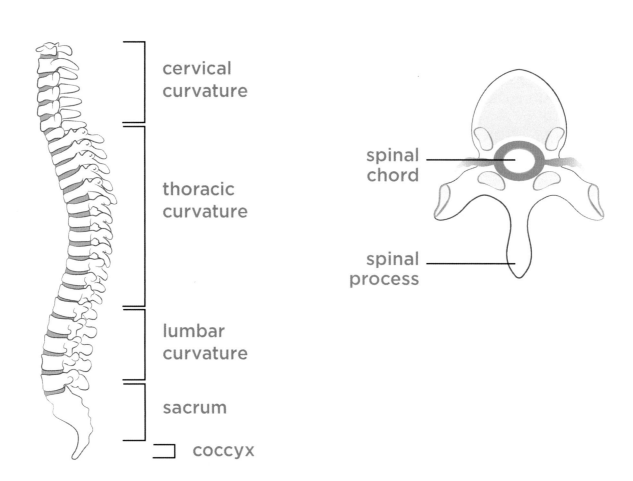

cervical
curvature

thoracic
curvature

lumbar
curvature

sacrum

coccyx

spinal
chord

spinal
process

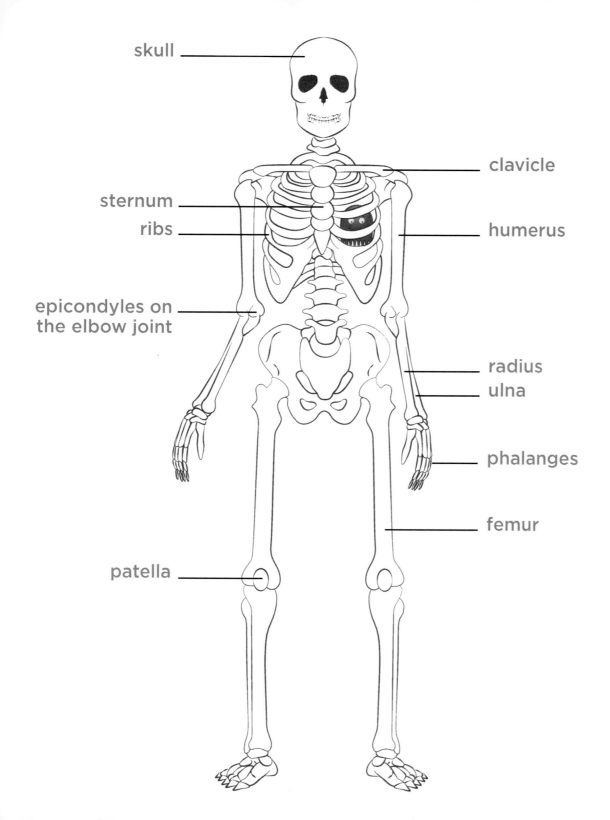

skull

clavicle

sternum

ribs

humerus

epicondyles on
the elbow joint

radius

ulna

phalanges

femur

patella

36.

What Do Your Bones Like To Eat?

The Human Body Detectives know that the bones need good healthy whole foods. Having strong bones means you can stand up straight, bend and twist, play sports, and protect your organs like the lungs and heart. Below are a few bone foods, but can you add a few others?

Remember in the story after the osteoid or bone matrix was laid down by the osteoblasts, the minerals calcium and phosphorus were needed to create new bone?

Great food calcium sources are:
Spinach
Kale (how about some kale chips?)
Broccoli
Almonds
Salmon
You can find calcium in many foods, not only dairy!

Great food phosphorus sources are:
Sunflower and pumpkin seeds
Soy beans (edamame)
Brazil and pine nuts
Organic natural peanut butter
Lentils

The mineral **magnesium** partners with calcium to form healthy bones. Almonds, cashews, millet and buckwheat all boost high levels of magnesium.

Vitamin D also plays a big role. We can get our vitamin D from the sun and from eating foods like fish, eggs and even mushrooms.

Remember, the best way to get all the nutrients you need is to color your plate with whole foods. Nuts, beans, whole grains, and fruits and vegetables are naturally abundant in nutrients essential to healthy bones.

How Do Your Bones Like To Move?

The Human Body Detectives know that the bones are living and need exercise as much as the heart does. Along with a healthy diet, physical activity is crucial for strong bones.

Do you like to run, hike, dance or even do yoga?
If so, your bones are happy, healthy and strong!

What physical movement did you do today to strengthen your bones?

Yoga	Soccer	Hike
Run	Baseball	Trampoline
Jog	Dance	Martial Arts
Swim	Gymnastics	Surf

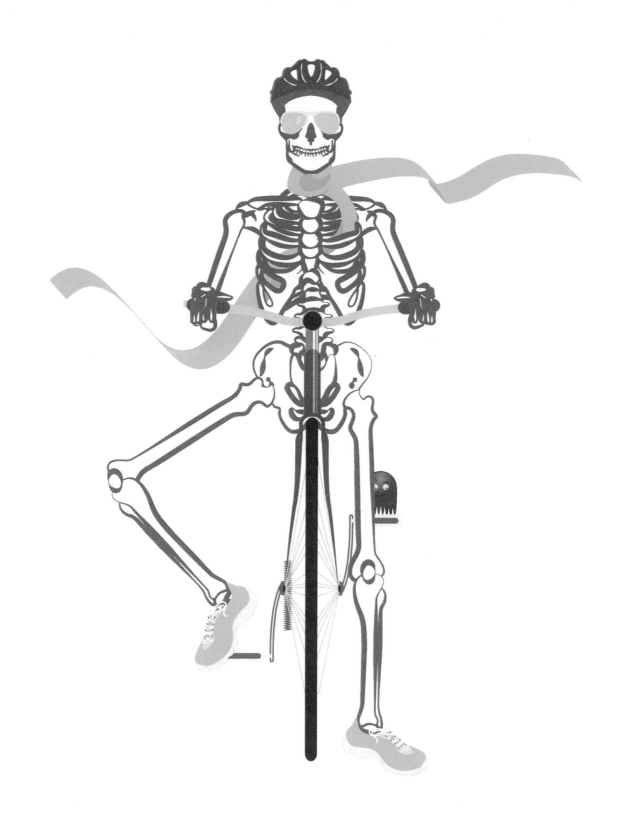

Jokes That Tickle Your Funny Bone

The Human Body Detectives love a great case, but they also love a funny joke! Here are some of Merrin and Pearl's favorites!

Do you have any?

What's a bone in your body that you can never break?
Your funny bone!

What do you call a skeleton who doesn't like to get up in the morning?
Lazy Bones.

Why does milk taste so good?
Because it has calci-YUM!

What did the skeleton say when his brother told a lie?
You can't fool me, I can see right through you.

What do skeletons say before they begin eating?
Bone appétit!

Why don't skeletons like to go to parties?
They have no body to dance with.

Why did the skeleton climb the tree?
Because the dog was after its bones.

Why wouldn't the skeleton go skydiving?
He didn't have the guts for it.

Why did the skeleton laugh?
Because he had a funny bone!

Why did the skeleton go disco dancing?
To see the boogy man.

Glossary

A list of useful skeletal words and their meaning.

Bone marrow (mair-oh) Bone marrow is a soft tissue found in the center of bones. Bone marrow has the important job of making blood cells.

Callus (cal-lus) The hematoma that forms due to a fracture will develop into a tougher tissue called a callus.

Cancellous bone (kan-sell-us) This bone is located inside compact bone and resembles a sponge. It is not quite as hard as compact bone, but it is still very strong.

Cartilage (kar-tel-ij): Bones in a baby are partly made of cartilage, which is soft and flexible. During childhood, as you are growing, the cartilage grows, too, and with the help of calcium and other minerals, will slowly be replaced by bone.

Cervical vertebrae (sir-vick-uhl VER-tuh-bray) The vertebra that makes up the neck.

Coccyx (COK-siks) The coccyx is the small bone, also referred to as the tailbone, at the base of the spine. It is made up of 4 bones that are fused together.

Collagen (col-a-gen) Collagen is a protein and is tough and strong. You can find collagen all over the body, in bones, ligaments, skin and tendons.

Compact bone (com-pact bone) Compact bone is located on the outer part of the bone that is very hard and smooth.

Costal cartilage (cost-tal kar-tel-ij) Costal cartilage is the flexible hyaline cartilage on the ribs that allows for easier breathing.

Epicondyle (epi-con-dyle) A projection on the surface of a bone, which is often an area for muscle and tendon attachment.

Fibroblast (fib-ro-blast) An immature fiber-producing cell made up of connective tissue and capable of turning into an osteoblast.

Fracture (frak-chur) A fracture is the separation or break of a bone.

Hematoma (he-ma-to-ma) A hematoma is a collection of blood cells due to an injury outside of a blood vessel.

Ligaments (LIH-guh-mints) Ligaments are fibrous and stretchy tissues that connect bones in the body.

Lumbar vertebrae (LUM-bar VER-tuh-bray) These are the 5 vertebrae between the rib cage and the pelvis.

Ossification (os-si-fi-ca-shun) Ossification is the process of laying down new bone, or it can also refer to when cartilage turns into solid bone.

Osteoblasts (os-te-o-blasts) Osteoblast cells are responsible for bone formation.

Osteoids (os-te-oids) Osteoids are referred to as the bone matrix. The osteoblasts secrete osteoids. Once calcium, zinc, phosphorus and other minerals become a part of the osteoid, new bone begins to form.

Parieto-temporal joint (par-EYE-ih-toh TEM-puh-rul) This is the junction between the parietal and temporal skull bones.

Periosteum (pare-ee-os-tee-um) Periosteum is located on the outer layer of bones. It's a thin, dense membrane that contains nerves and blood vessels that nourish the bone. It is in between the skin and the bone.

Sacrum (SAY-krum) The sacrum is located below the lumbar vertebrae and is made up of 5 vertebrae that are fused together to form a single bone.

Spinal cord (spin-nal cord) Your spinal cord is part of your nervous system. It makes sure important messages can get to and from your brain. Your vertebrae keep the spinal cord safe.

Spinal process (spin-nal pro-cess) The spinal process is the bony projection from the vertebrae that you feel when someone runs their fingers down your spine. They are important for muscle and ligament attachment.

Sternum (STUR-num) The sternum is located in the middle of your chest and is commonly referred to as the breastbone.

Synovial fluid (SIH-no-vee-ul) This fluid is special joint fluid that allows your joints to move freely.

Thoracic vertebrae (thuh-RAS-ick VER-tuh-bray) The 12 thoracic vertebrae are located below the cervical vertebrae.

Vertebrae (VER-tuh-bray) The vertebrae make up 33 bones in humans. Each one is shaped like a ring (7 are the cervical, 12 are the thoracic, 5 are the lumbar, 5 are fused bones that form the sacrum, and the last 4 are fused bones that form the coccyx or tailbone).

I AM GRATEFUL

This HBD journey has been filled with excitement and passion and I am very appreciative to my friends, family, colleagues and all of my customers who have supported me during this crazy fun venture. Thank you Thank you!

I also need to bow my head to Nina Jones (jonesy.ca) who has been with me from the beginning, adding her magic touch in layout and formatting; Jessica Swift, Swift Ink Editorial Services, for her genius editing; and SF300 for creating the exact images I have wanted for each book. I could not ask for a better group of people to work with.

Now, on to the next HBD book... stay tuned!

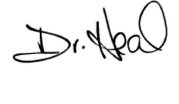

Dr. Heather is a practicing naturopathic physician who promotes wellness and naturopathic healthcare on her website **drheathernd.com**. She is also the author of the award winning book series, **Human Body Detectives**. Dr. Heather lives on the Big Island of Hawaii with her husband and two daughters, and is currently at work on the next **Human Body Detectives** adventure.

Ebook apps of the **Human Body Detectives** books: *Battle with the Bugs, The Lucky Escape* and *A Heart Pumping Adventure*, are available on iTunes.

THE ELEMENTARY CURRICULUM IS AVAILABLE ON THESE SITES:

Homeschool Buyers Co op: **homeschoolbuyersco-op.org**
Teachers pay Teachers: **teacherspayteachers.com**
as well as **humanbodydetectives.com**

Visit the **Human Body Detectives** website for free downloads, to view the HBD book trailers, and to watch Human Body Detectives Merrin and Pearl in the kitchen and visiting exciting places!

 visit us on Facebook:
facebook.com/HumanBodyDetectives

 tweet with Dr. Heather on Twitter:
twitter.com/drheathernd

LOOK FOR OTHER BOOKS IN THE HUMAN BODY DETECTIVE SERIES:

The Lucky Escape
Battle with the Bugs
A Heart Pumping Adventure

52992123R00033

Made in the USA
Lexington, KY
23 September 2019